AF386547

Golem Soveticus:
Prigov as Brecht and
Warhol in One Persona

Aleksandr Skidan
Translated by Kevin M.F. Platt

Preamble

Dmitri Alexandrovich Prigov was a poet: "the last great poet of the Soviet era."[*][1] But his true significance is greater, far greater, than that. Which is not to say that Prigov isn't interesting as a "Soviet phenomena": in the way that his undertakings' multifaceted, all-encompassing, titanic universalism enables a clarification, perhaps even a wholesale reconceptualization, of the "Soviet era," and of the "Soviet" itself. In my view, however, Prigov's most interesting features lie altogether elsewhere.

Prigov carried out a revolution in the poetic means of production comparable to the industrial revolution: his logico–poetic machines displaced the "human labor" of traditional lyric expression—of handmade lyricism, so to speak. (Prigov himself liked to call it "artistic handicraft.") Prigov's work presented not just a new form of poetics—it gave us a new form of poeisis. It was founded on an instrumentalization of poetic technologies in order to reroute them towards extra- or meta-poetic tasks—for instance, investigation of the logical construction and formal premises of various categories of utterance (artistic, scientific, religious, theoretical, ideological, etc.). In effect, the text was transformed into a kind of logarithmic table.[2]

To approach Prigov in this way is to position him in global historical context. This is a crucial step. It also explains his violent rejection by those who view poetry as the

* This was the title of one of the first published reactions to D. A. Prigov's death.

self-expression of a lyric subject identical with itself, of a deep "I" with privileged access to true being. That conception of poetry corresponds to a preindustrial era—one that hadn't yet experienced the alienation, objectification and automatization of labor processes. To my mind, in Prigov these "machine bottlenecks" and the "logistics" of their management are the crux of the matter. That is: this is not simply the poet's comic, deflationary play with ideological and/or poetic clichés, nor even his (de)mystification of "the Russian religious-apocalyptic consciousness."

Of course, it's impossible to overlook carnival laughter in Prigov's work. And it, too, provoked misunderstanding and hostility. "A rampaging graphomaniac," "sacrilege," "insolence and Satanism": these are the defensive reactions of a *unidimensionally serious* cultural consciousness, dogmatically defending the "miracle and authority" of the elevated tradition against any overly presumptuous commerce with it.[3] Nevertheless, this indisputably important aspect of Prigov's activities must be seen as secondary in relation to his truly subversive industrial-serial technology of cultural production.

A few more preliminary remarks: don't let the title of this work confuse you. I certainly don't want to propose that Dmitri Alexandrovich Prigov (DAP) just adapted or appropriated Brecht's and Warhol's techniques. To the contrary, I will demonstrate that DAP, in classic manner, absolutely à la russe, synthesized their (obviously, completely distinct) strategies, applying them to poetic construction. Why "à la russe" and why "in classic manner"? Because in Russia, at least since Peter the Great, imported Western cultural models have consistently assumed unrecognizable, altered forms. Furthermore, one may propose that it is precisely this deformation of foreign "originals" that constitutes the primordial—and much pursued, since it lies on the very surface—content of "native Russian culture." Primary examples in this regard include Lomonosov, who installed our versification system according to German models, and Pushkin, who consecrated our modern national tradition by grafting on French and English literary forms. And didn't the authentic, "great and mighty"* Russian language itself arise thanks only to translation?

The parallels with Andy Warhol are obvious. I'm thinking not only of his serial method or of the Factory, which resemble DAP's "Stakhanovite," production-line assembly of poetic texts (36000 poems is an absolute world record!),† but also of the overall transformation of the aesthetic paradigm that is rightfully attributed to Andy Warhol.[4] To be precise: Warhol shifted the center of artistic activity from the work of art to artistic behavior as calculated strategy.

* Ivan Turgenev eulogized the "great and mighty, righteous and free Russian language," in one of his 1882 "poems in prose." Subsequently, the phrase "great and mighty Russian language" became proverbial (in other words, a cliché).[KP]

† Even if the figure, which was calculated by Igor Smirnov, is exaggerated, possibly the only rival to Prigov in the field of poetic shock-work is Evtushenko, who was also a personality of truly multifarious talents, a pop-figure of the preceding era, although he was admittedly distinct from Prigov in his "savage seriousness" and utter lack of a distanced vantage point on his own socio-cultural role. (Compare, for instance, Baudelaire, situated at the origins of European modernism, who wrote slightly more than 200 poems in all.)

Prigov's adaptation and reconceptualization of this epochal transformation enabled him to assume a meta-poetic, meta-aesthetic position in any field of creativity, rendering it a consciously articulated cultural politics. Warhol's serial method (*Triple Elvis, 80 Two-Dollar Bills, Front and Rear, White Car Crash Nineteen Times, Four Jackies*, and so on) first demonstrated with absolute lucidity the paradox Walter Benjamin sought to grasp in "The Work of Art in the Age of Mechanical Reproducibility." The contemporary Russian poet and critic Dmitry Golynko-Wolfson evokes this same paradox with his assertion that "Prigov proved that today, original utterances arise primarily out of the principle of serial repetition."[5]

Things may appear less obvious regarding Brecht. Yet on closer examination Prigov and the German poet and reformer of the theater share at least two foundational principles (attentive study yields many more). First of all, there is the *Verfremdungseffekt*, the "Alienation Effect," derived from the Russian Formalist idea of making-strange or *ostrananie.** Yet in distinction from the Formalists, Brecht's Alienation Effect was directed not just toward deautomatization of perception, but also toward the interruption of aesthetic illusion as a form of "false consciousness." The actor in Brechtian theater, rather than being transformed

* Brecht's term "Verfremdungseffekt," commonly translated as "Alienation Effect," should not be associated overly closely with the Marxist conception of "alienation," corresponding to Marx's etymologically related, yet distinct German term "entfremdung. A more precise translation might be "Estrangement Effect" (evoking the Russian Formalist influence on Brecht's thinking) or "Distancing Effect" (that echoes the common French translation of Brecht's term).

into one of the play's characters, presents the character from a position of critical distance. Similarly, in his texts DAP continuously "steps out of his role," baring the artificiality, the fabricated nature of textual construction, along with the lyric subject's constructed nature (its "character-ness"). Both Brecht and Prigov rely on the audience's rational, analytical capabilities, rather than methods of suggestion, hypnosis and empathy. When identification and hypnosis do occur, they are deployed in an exaggerated, parodic key (as "theater in theater").

Furthermore, for Brecht and Prigov alike, this self-reflexive analytical technique becomes a tool for the presentation and crystallization of dominant ideology, insofar as it speaks through conventional artistic forms and discourses. In Brecht's case, of course, this was a bourgeois ideology that was diffused into "aesthesis," whereas it was primarily communist (utopian, messianic) for Prigov. Nevertheless, given that we are witness at present to a capitalist cultural industrialization and the triumph of a new utopia—the utopia of consumption—DAP's synthesis has vital contemporary significance.*

* Let us note here one additional, not insignificant distinction between Prigov and Brecht. The former's strategy closely approaches what is referred to in the contemporary art world as "subversive affirmation": an undermining support (or a dethroning confirmation), based on hyperidentification with the form of discourse that is reproduced. This grants Prigov's poetry a certain additional equivocal charm that Brecht lacks. So in the cycle about the "Policeman," DAP "enters into" his character to such a degree that his exaggerated identification (hyperidentification) is practically impossible to distinguish from the author's sincerest admiration and even love for him.

Warhol, or Apology for the Machine

Warhol: Someone said that Brecht wanted everybody to think alike. I want everybody to think alike. But Brecht wanted to do it through Communism, in a way. Russia is doing it under government. It's happening here all by itself without being under a strict government; so if it's working without trying, why can't it work without being Communist? Everybody looks alike and acts alike, and we're getting more and more that way. I think everybody should be a machine. I think everybody should like everybody.
Swenson: Is that what Pop Art is all about?
Warhol: Yes. It's liking things.
Swenson: And liking things is like being a machine?
Warhol: Yes, because you do the same thing every time. You do it over and over again.[6]

The chief thing is to learn to think bluntly. Blunt thinking is great thinking. Politics is the pursuit of business by unbusiness-like methods.
—Bertolt Brecht, *Threepenny Novel*[7]

In his innumerable lectures and interviews, as well as in the "advisory notes" that preface many of his works, DAP never tires of emphasizing the priority of the mode of artistic behavior over the work of art or the text. His final interview before his death (April 16, 2007) is titled "Art today is concerned not with content, but with new forms of artistic behavior."[8] I'll cite two characteristic statements: "Let's note once more that poetry is not only texts, but also a particular mode for construction and presentation to society of significant forms of cultural behavior—poetic behavior, in the present case";[9] "It's precisely on the level of behavioral models that fundamental problems are resolved and something is affirmed. And what is affirmed is, of course, freedom. Indeed, our times and this kind of culture have rendered the problem of freedom crucially important. The problem of human rights can be reformulated as the attempt to free the personality from collective dictates. The same thing is happening in art. It addresses the possibility of the artist's freedom from the languages looming over him, which represent collectivities and nothing else—the collective experience of the past."[10] DAP worked with historical epochs, socio-cultural paradigms, and forms of consciousness. His terminology recalls least of all the language of a poet (as it is usually understood) or even a literary scholar. Instead, Prigov's language is the scientistic sociolect of a student of social processes—one who, on the basis of objective regularities, makes conjectures and articulates an understanding of art and his own place in it. The poetic *function* is radically historicized, placed in a broad socio-cultural, political context (e.g. the problem of freedom). Indeed, it is *derived* from this context.

DAP consistently identified visual art as the center of both contemporary cultural production and of his own development. To Sergey Shapoval's question, "What has influenced you most in cultural life?" DAP answers without hesitation "Visual art. I was far more advanced in visual art than in literature. At some point I just began wondering: is there a version of the Sots-Art* and

* Sots-Art was a mode of unofficial conceptualist art that appeared on the Soviet underground scene in the 1970s. It was oriented on the parodic deflation of official Soviet culture and political language. The term is a mash-up of "Pop Art" and "socialism." [KP]

conceptualist mentality in literature? I began to search for analogues."[11]

I set out in search of analogues, too, and couldn't not think of Andy Warhol. Warhol might well have reformulated the assertion of Brecht's character, included above as an epigraph, as something like "Art is the pursuit of commerce by other means." That might sound blasphemous. But isn't it true that Warhol's stenciled serial works blaspheme against the great artists of the past—Leonardo da Vinci, but also, in a different way, Marcel Duchamp—eliminating or obviating the border between original and copy, unique and mass produced, avant-garde and kitsch, and ultimately between artworks and consumer goods? As Harold Rosenberg noted, not without sarcasm, "The innovation of Andy Warhol consists not in his paintings, but in his version of the comedy of the artist as a public figure. 'Andy' [...] has carried the ongoing de-definition of art to the point at which nothing is left of art but the fiction of the artist."[12] Actually, it was Duchamp who began the process of the "de-definition" of art, also not without notes of comedy, as early as his Dada period, when he moved from easel painting to his quasi-scientific experiments ("stoppages") and "ready-mades" (mass consumer goods, which, transported into the exhibit space, acquired a novel non-utilitarian function). Nevertheless, the new model of artistic behavior that DAP inherited was constituted by the founding father of "popism." This model may legitimately be termed a "strategy," since it presupposes the intentional articulation of interrelationships not only with a particular artform's dominant styles and movements, but also with their programmatic resources—in other words, with the "superstructure": advertisement, market, mass media, cultural institutions, the entire public sphere, including consumption. Put another way, activity in the field of art, with its immanent logic, hierarchy of names, balance of forces and so on, is supplemented by and enters into dependence on ostensibly extra-artistic factors. Linguists would say that the pragmatics of (speech) behavior becomes the dominant, leading to the radical reconstruction of semantics and syntax, which undergo deformation and are pushed into the background.

Warhol became a star of the first magnitude on the American art scene and the leading showman of art. For his part, Prigov was the one representative of uncensored, unofficial poetry of the Soviet era to achieve general recognition and popular adulation. In post-Soviet space he became a unique pop-figure, continuously present in mass media, like a show business personality, a movie star, or a politician. Prigov was interviewed and featured frequently on television as an "expert" on the most varied questions. No other artist or poet of his generation could boast of anything similar.

DAP and Warhol also converge in their improbable productivity. Just one example: in less than half a year, from August to December of 1965, Warhol created two thousand paintings and actively participated in the production of more than seventy films in the Factory. Prigov's world record (36000 poems!) has already been mentioned; but additionally, he is the author of stories, plays, nearly a hundred alphabet books, novels, installations, and drawings. "I have a quota: I need to write at least two poems a day; I need to draw every day."[13] Furthermore, both were Renaissance men, who engaged in all kinds of activity with equal success. Warhol made his mark not only as an art innovator, but also as a designer and collector, the organizer of an unusual production commune (the Factory), a film director, producer, and musician who played a cardinal role in the emergence of The Velvet Underground, a publisher (of the journal *Interview*), patron, music video director, and author (of two books: *The Philosophy of Andy Warhol (From A to B and Back Again)* and *POPism: The Warhol Sixties*).

Prigov performed with no less brilliance on the "interdisciplinary" stage: poetry, prose, essays in cultural studies, painting, graphic work, actions, performances (including video-performances), collaborations with jazz and rock musicians as well as with composers from the academic avant-garde, participation in media-operas; and he made a name for himself as an actor (in the films *Taxi Blues*, *Khrustalev, My Car!*, and *Enthusiast's Highway*).

But "encyclopedism" and pragmatics (in the linguistic sense) do not exhaust their resemblances. Let's return to the question of the profanation, or devaluation, of the original. Historians of Pop Art observe that at the end of the 1950s, the explorations of Robert Rauschenberg, Jasper Johns, and Roy Lichtenstein extended far beyond those of Warhol, who still betrayed "the stigma of the commercial artist."[14] The turning point arrives at the start of the 1960s, when Warhol takes up silk-screen and the reproduction of media images, along with the representation of mass consumer goods. "Photographic silkscreen ... offered several advantages. It allowed Warhol to get rid of any handmade elements in his pictures, entirely to remove any subjectivity and thus finally to free himself from the clutch of Abstract Expressionism."[15] "The artist of everyday life" (this, with a nod to Baudelaire, was the name of a 2005 Warhol exhibition at the Tretyakov Gallery) began literally stamping out paintings in industrial manner based on newspaper photographs, using a stencil on mesh, achieving dizzying stereotypographic effects either via variations in color or the doubling of the drawing's line, simultaneously putting reality to death and endlessly reproducing it—"cloning" it. From the principle of serial repetition, a new type of "aura"— machinic or profane—was born, one that corresponded to the era of mechanical reproducibility and electronic mass media. Long before this, Baudelaire had brought to light the paradoxical dialectic of original and copy, writing in his diary "I must create a cliché" ("Je dois creér un poncif").[16] Musing on Baudelaire's behavior on the literary market, which starts to assume the character of an "objective force" by the mid nineteenth century and the industrial revolution, Walter Benjamin notes, "Baudelaire was perhaps the first to conceive of a market-oriented originality, which for that very reason was more original in its day than any other."[17]

At the end of the 1960s and start of the 1970s, Prigov's situation was in some ways similar to Warhol's—with the obvious caveat that, although competition in the artistic sphere did exist, there was no market in the Western sense in the Soviet Union. The role of mass culture was performed on one hand by ideology, and on the other by its surrogate (or side product): classical Russian and world culture, worked over by censorship procedures until it gained the character of a "common place." In the 1960s, Prigov wrote respectable yet frankly derivative poetry in the style of Zabolotsky, Akhmatova, or Mandelstam.[18] The poets of the Lianozovo school—in particular Vsevolod Nekrasov, but also Eduard Limonov in a different way—were clearly more advanced than Prigov in their "conceptualist research." In the essay "Graphomania as Device (Lebyadkin, Khlebnikov, Limonov and others)," Alexander Zholkovsky offers two eloquent quotations from Limonov at the end of the 1960s that can be read as textual precursors of the mature Prigov:

* * *

My friends, insulted and enraged,
Curse the state's unholy power
But adopting a sort of Indian stance
I think: what's it to me?

Can it stop me having babies
or breeding ducks out on the river
and can it stop the philosophizing
of my friends, this power of the state?...

* * *

The state is certainly awful
But it alone, indeed
Can help me deal with you
For it there is real need[19]

It was only after he came to terms with his own "imitativeness," and then with "imitativeness" as such—the inherent reproducibility of poetic subjectivity—transforming it into the poem's constructive principle, that Prigov was able to become "Dmitri Alexandrovich Prigov, Academician of Belyaevo." Just as Warhol took the elements of mass production, comics, advertisements, brand labels, photos from mass periodicals, and so on as his material, DAP utilized Soviet ideological discourse in its most profane, "domesticated" form (a taboo move for prior unofficial artists), as well as various socio-cultural fetishes, or "brands" ("Pushkin," "Chaikovsky," the "Policeman," "Moscow," etc.). Despite their cynical manipulativeness, or possibly precisely because of it, Warhol's techniques lay bare and bring to the surface the occult mechanisms of consumerist society, mirroring back to the public the secret of its commodity fetishism. In Warhol's work, the euphoria of consumption rhymes with anesthesia, effacement, and death. The distinctive feature of DAP's mechanized, industrial-serial method is a comparable duality, transposed from visual to textual production and reoriented towards (post-)Soviet society and ideology.

To be fair, we should also identify DAP's more distant predecessors in the realm of poetry proper. The creation of "logarithmic machines," engaging mechanisms of iteration, can be found among the Dadaists (Kurt Schwitters' "merz machines" or, again, Duchamp's literary puns), the Surrealists (the collective game of the "exquisite corpse"— automatic writing intended as a stenography of free association), the members of Oberiu, who worked with various kinds of folklore, the Oulipo authors (in particular Jacques Roubaud, whose book of sonnets *Epsilon* licenses the generation of a potentially unlimited number of additional poems), William Burroughs with his cut-up treatment of found texts, John Cage, and Jackson Mac Low.

Still earlier there was Lautréamont (Isidore Ducasse), who announced that "personal poetry has had its moment of juggling with the relative and contorting with the contingent. Let us take up again the indestructible thread of impersonal poetry."[20] By way of Raymond Roussel, this thread leads back to Ramon Llull (and in general to the tradition of Kabbalistic writing over the centuries, including Rabbi Loew and his Golem) and to the prayer drums that replaced Buddhist monks' collective chanting of mantras. Yet DAP went further, subordinating this simultaneously ludic and sacral combinatorics to cognitive, logico-analytic—strictly speaking, extra-poetic—tasks: "In art I work not with metaphysics, but with logic and epistemology—if such terms can be applied to an artistic-creative gesture—with the correlation of any utterance against the simple probability of its appearance, of its discovery, against its truth; with the proof or negation of its right to exist."[21]

Brecht, or Against Neutralization

> What makes Brecht's enterprise exemplary is that it takes
> more risks than others: Brecht proceeds to the extreme of
> a certain meaning (which we may call, roughly, a Marxist
> meaning), but precisely when it "takes" (solidifies into a
> positive signified) he suspends this meaning as a ques-
> tion (a suspension we encounter in the particular quality of
> historical time represented in Brecht's theater, a time of the
> not-yet). This very subtle friction between a (fulfilled) mean-
> ing and a (suspended) signification is an enterprise which
> far surpasses, in audacity, in difficulty, in necessity, too, the
> suspension of meaning which the avant-garde believed it had
> produced by a pure subversion of ordinary language and of
> theatrical conformism.
> —Roland Barthes, "Literature and Signification"[22]

Out of Bertolt Brecht's vast creative legacy—and he was
the author of plays, poetry, prose, pamphlets, essays, tracts,
instructional manuals, and social-political commentaries,
obeying an imperative already familiar to us: "Thou shalt
produce"[23]—I will focus on his concept of epic (non-Aris-
totelian) theater. Even more narrowly: let us consider his
innovative techniques for the actor's stage presence, which
intersect at a number of points with DAP's poetic techniques and with his habitus or strategy more broadly. As
was the case with Warhol, my proposals concern not influence or borrowing, but rather a structural homology.

Brecht described the principles of epic theater and his
distinctive acting techniques in a series of theoretical
works of the late 1930s and 1940s. These works: "Theater

for Pleasure or Theater for Instruction" (1936), "New Technique of Acting" (1940), "The Messingkauf Dialogues" (or "Buying Brass") (1939-1940), "Short Organum for the Theatre" (1949), and others appeared in the fifth volume of Brecht's collected works in Russian translation, published in the USSR in 1963-65 (this was also the moment of his peak popularity, and coincided with Prigov's slow, still latent development as an author). Yet one may already observe elements of the phenomenon that Brecht would later term the "Alienation effect" or "A-effect" (*Verfremdungseffekt* or *V-effekt*) in his early dramatic experiments (the plays *Baal* and *Drums in the Night*) and poetry (the collection *Domestic Breviary*, 1927). Symptomatically, they take shape from devices of parody and "plagiarism" (the reworking, refashioning, or contamination of others' texts).[*24] *Domestic Breviary*, for instance, parodies religious psalms and hymns, didactic urban romances from the repertoires of street singers and organ grinders, as well as lyrics by Goethe and Schiller, popular to the point of cliché. Brecht fills these "virtuous and respectable" forms with "rollicking, wild, either intentionally naïve or provocatively cynical tales of criminals and the depraved, patricides and filicides, pirates and gold-diggers."[25] The hero of these ballads is a *sui generis* theatrical (verbal) mask: a man about town and immoralist who mouths off with a frank absence of shame about things that the upstanding bourgeois would prefer to hide behind an elevated phrase.

* See Brecht's polemical note/mockery "On Plagiarism," in which he announces his intention (if only it weren't an "inopportune moment") to take up his "old plan ... to honour literary plagiarism and to reinvest it with its old accustomed rights."

Later, Brecht will operate both more subtly and more crudely (more audaciously, Barthes would say): taking up the plots of Sophocles, Shakespeare, Schiller and other classic authors, he rewrites them in order to provoke, with mimicry and an exaggerated reproduction of familiar rhetoric, a collision between "meaning" and "signification," establishing critical distance in relation to the source text. Brecht's "plagiarisms" or "palimpsests" step decisively towards the secularization of literature, the hybridization of the original and the demolition of the "aura" (of authenticity) derived, as Benjamin explained, from art's ritual, cultic function.* Brecht understands literary material literally—which is to say, in a materialist manner, as a means of production to be brought under collective control.

This is a materialist aesthetics of laughter, of "casting down." Brecht founds his verbal art on incessant ambivalences, witticisms, cynicism, mockery, and on the "low" element that he punningly correlates with commitment to the social depths. Punning thought is the thought of the clown. And one senses in Prigov the continual presence of the ambivalent, carnival-square word, profaning, dethroning, and returning "elevated," "sacral" meanings to earth. At the same time, Prigov's masquerade includes,

* In "The Work of Art in the Age of Mechanical Reproducibility," Benjamin refers only once to Brecht—and in a footnote, at that. Yet his ideas permeate the essay in obvious manner—in particular, his thought concerning art's changed function when it is transformed into a commercial ware, on one hand, and under the pressure of mass distribution and reproduction, on the other.

as a rule, a supplementary level—a level of self-irony (a romantic trope).*[26] Yet rather than parodying any poetic stance in particular, Prigov instead articulates a parody of the mechanism of cultural production (*poeisis*) as such. In so doing, he *sends up* and *places on display* the "vulgar" logic of relations of production that elevated rhetoric (the rhetoric of the sublime) disavows. Consider how this process unfolds in the "Second Banal Treatise on the Theme: Being Famous Is Not Beautiful"†:

When you're, let's say, famous
Being famous is not beautiful
But if you're unfamous
Then being famous is not only
Desirable, but also beautiful
For beauty isn't the result
Of your hypothetical fame
But fame is the result

* Friedrich Schlegel comprehends romantic irony, heir to Socratic irony, as "entirely involuntary and nevertheless completely conscious dissimulation (*Verstellung*)." "It contains and incites a feeling of the insoluble conflict of the absolute and the relative, of the impossibility and the necessity of total communication. It is the freest of all liberties, for it enables us to rise above our own self; and still the most legitimate, for it is absolutely necessary. It is a good sign if the harmonious dullards fail to understand this constant self-parody, if over and over again they believe and disbelieve until they become giddy and consider jest to be seriousness and seriousness to be jest."

† Prigov's poem playfully responds to a well-known (and somewhat preachy) poem by Boris Pasternak, that begins with the line "Being famous is not beautiful."[KP]

Of beauty, and beauty will save the world!
But sure, being famous is not beautiful
When you're already famous.[27]

Prigov's text contaminates not only Pasternak and Dostoevsky (and who really remembers that the sacramental phrase about beauty belongs not to the venerable Fedor Mikhailovich, but to his character?), but also Ian Satunovsky, who evokes Pushkin in turn*:

Do I desire posthumous fame?
Hah!
What other fame can I desire?
[...]
Do I pass time with mindless youths?
I do!
Though I'd prefer to pass on doing time.[28]

But let's return to the theater. Brecht's theory and practice is founded on the Alienation Effect, which can easily be confused with Marx's etymologically related term "alienation" (*Entfremdung*). To clarify the distinction, we may consider the Alienation Effect in theater, where it is expressed via a number of distinct devices. Consider Patrice Pavis' account, which I will expand with certain necessary additions [in brackets]:

* Satunovsky's poem plays off of well-known poems by Pushkin, Russia's national poet, one of which predicts his posthumous fame, and the other of which includes the line "Do I pass time with mindless youth."[KP]

1. The *fabula* tells two stories: one is concrete and the other is an abstract and metaphorical parable of it. [Or it's more contemporary variation. Brecht frequently takes up well-known plots, placing their "form" and "content" in irreconcilable conflict.]

2. The *scenery* presents the object to be recognized (e.g. a factory) and the criticism to be made (exploitation of workers). [It does not depict, but rather schematically refers to one or another topic or space.]

3. *Gestures* provide information about the individual and his social status and relationship with the working world, his *gestus*.*

4. The *diction* does not "psychologize" the text by trivializing it, but restores rhythm and artificial construction (e.g. musical delivery of the alexandrine).

5. Through his *acting*, the actor shows the character he plays, rather than incarnating him.

6. *Addresses to the audience*, songs and visible scenery changes are also devices which break the illusion. [Also: the introduction of film clips, titles and other commentaries on the action.]

7-8. [And we may add: Rejection of the division into acts in favor of a "montage" of episodes and scenes, as well as rejection of the central figure (protagonist) around which classical theater is constructed (decentering of structure).][29]

These devices are encountered individually in ancient Greek, Chinese, Shakespearean and Chekhovian theater, not to mention the theatrical productions of Brecht's

* Brecht uses the term "Gestus" to refer to the embodied reality of social relations.[KP]

contemporaries Piscator (with whom he collaborated), Meyerhold, Vakhtangov, Eisenstein (about which he knew), and agitprop. Brecht's key innovation was the systematization of his predecessors' and contemporaries' strategies into a dominant aesthetic principle, allowing him to elaborate a self-reflexive artistic language. In the context of the theater, this means the intentional "baring of the device" and the "showing of showing."

Brecht didn't arrive immediately at alienation's political implications, just as he didn't come to the term itself until later. First it was necessary to gain knowledge about Marxist theory (via Karl Korsch) and the Russian Formalist "estrangement" (via Sergey Tretyakov).[30] Yet as early as the start of the 1920s Brecht adopted a stance of uncompromising belligerence towards bourgeois theater, condemning its soporific, hypnotic effect that transforms the public into a passive object (in Munich, as Brecht began his career, National Socialism was just gaining force, with its demagoguery and magical, gestural magnetism, bordering on esotericism). Brecht referred to this theater as "cookery" and "a branch of the bourgeois trade in narcotics."

In his search for antidotes Brecht arrived at a recognition of the principal distinction between two forms of theater: dramatic (Aristotelian) and epic. Dramatic theater seeks to subjugate spectators' emotions, leading them to surrender "with their entire being" to the action on the stage, and in so doing to lose their grasp on the boundary between theatrical spectacle and reality. The result: purgation of affect (as if under hypnosis) and reconciliation (with destiny, fate, "the human condition," the eternal and unchanging). Epic theater, in contrast, appeals to spectators' analytical capacities, awakening doubt and questioning, impelling them toward recognition of the historically conditioned social relations that stand behind any given conflict. The result: critical catharsis, the *consciousness of unconsciousness* (the "consciousness the audience must have of the unconsciousness prevailing on the stage"[31]), and a desire to change the course of events (not on stage—in reality). Epic theater, which is Brecht's theater, absorbs the critical, metalinguistic function usually reserved for philosophy, art criticism, or critical theory, becoming a self-critique of art by art's own means.

Over time, Brecht's innovations have been neutralized by the theater industry, which has transformed them into one set of theatrical conventions among others, torn away from any methodology or radical program of questioning spectacle as spectacle (a task that is taken up again later by the Situationist International and Godard's cinema). A similar neutralization threatens Prigov, who is often viewed reductively as poet-satirist of "Soviet ideological discourse." Regardless of this description's diverse implications in the hands of various critics, it overlooks his "murderous consistency of formal cognition" in relation to any form of utterance—poetic, artistic, scholarly, religious, and so on. As Prigov said in an interview with Igor Sid: "My linguistic activity is an effort to demonstrate to the individual and to society that all of these conventional systems are not truths from heaven. That they operate within definite limits... This is one of the modest tasks of the sort of activity I pursue: to bring to light the

limits outside of which language becomes non-criterial
and totalitarian."[32] In light of this threat (and in the case
of Brecht, neutralization is simply an established fact), I
propose that we directly engage the German playwright's
theoretical legacy.

In the treatise-manual "New Technique of Acting," Brecht
explicitly articulates the preconditions and primary objective of the A-effect:

> The first condition for the achievement of the A-effect
> is that the actor must invest what he has to show with a
> definite *gestus* of showing. [...] Once the idea of total trans-
> formation is abandoned the actor speaks his part not as if he
> were improvising it himself but like a quotation. At the same
> time he obviously has to render all the quotation's overtones,
> the remark's full human and concrete shape; similarly the
> gesture he makes must have the full substance of a human
> gesture, even though it now represents a copy.
>
> [...] The attitude which he adopts is a socially critical one.
> In his exposition of the incidents and in his characterization
> of the person he tries to bring out those features which come
> within society's sphere. In this way his performance becomes
> a discussion (about social conditions) with the audience he is
> addressing.
>
> [...] The object of the A-effect is to alienate the social
> *gestus* underlying every incident. By social *gestus* is meant
> the mimetic and gestural expression of the social relation-
> ships prevailing between people of a given period.[33]

Or consider another formulation that sounds like a
straightforward commentary on DAP's technique:

To achieve the A-effect the actor must give up his *complete conversion* into the stage character. He *shows* the character, he *quotes* his lines, he *repeats* a real-life incident. The audience is not entirely "carried away"; it need not conform psychologically, adopt a fantastic attitude towards fate as portrayed. [...] The incidents are *historicized* and socially *set*. (The former, of course, occurs above all with present-day incidents: whatever is is not always, and will not always be so. The latter repeatedly casts a questionable light on the prevailing social order and subjects it to discussion.) [italics in the original][34]

Let's compare two Prigov poems:

Just a little more—
When as one half-dead, damned at the threshold,
Like an insect, like one carried away,
I look back with such mortal force—
That the centriciput axis splits
That rock cries out and the beast carries off the child.

(1963)

Come, my flute, out in the dust and heat,
Sweetheart of the First Cavalry, and the Second,
Play a tune for us—something otherworldly
To rise above our heads up to the heavens.

Sing to us about diversions of war
Or perhaps a fearsome labor stunt
The beasts will listen and the grass stand tall
And men will lie down at the front

(1980)

Both poems[35] play out eschatological scenes related to the Orpheus myth—to art's magical potential to transform and renovate the world. (According to myth, Orpheus's song entranced even wild animals.) Yet the first differs from the second in the same way that dramatic theater, with its demand for impersonation, for complete identification with the role, differs from Brechtian epic theater. In "Just a little more…" there is no verbal mask, no distance between the author and the subject of the utterance: the perspective of author and lyric persona coincide. And although in the first poem the reader might sense allusions to Akhmatova ("I look back with such mortal force") or to Mandelstam (the "centriciput axis"), the second poem is written in its entirety as a *citation* and presents what is no longer an existential, but rather a "social" theatrical *gestus* in Brecht's sense—which is to say a *historicizing gestus*, laying bare the mythopoetic matrix and its ideological undercarriage.

Brecht's politicization of theater practice (which "repeatedly casts a questionable light on the prevailing social order") and his conception of critical catharsis correspond to Prigov's understanding of his "cultural-critical" mission: "…I want to defend the possibility of rejecting subordination to any and all totalizing ideas and ideologies. All viewpoints aspire to truth, but my object is to reveal each viewpoint not as a truth, but as a form of conventionality."[36] "Working with conceptualism, we were locked in a harsh opposition with the state as bearer of utopia. Our consciousness was of a cultural-critical nature: we subjected not only utopia and the state institutions responsible for its reproduction to critique, but furthermore all linguistic totalizations, which were chiefly linked to state language."[37] Prigov's critical position extended not only to the language of state, but potentially to that of the mass media, to cultural mythologies, to liberal free-market ideology and its derivatives: "As a starting point I take Parkinson's law, which says that any language in the course of its development will aspire to exceed its own limits and to become a totalitarian language of description. This is my fundamental premise. I don't go burning books by Akhmatova. Rather, I carry out a specific cultural procedure. Put simply, I work within the bounds of culture. *You could say I manifest a technology of consciousness of a new type, one that is already banal in the context of world culture*, but which is still startling and fearsome here" (my italics—AS).[38]

Brecht, in similar fashion, didn't burn Aristotle's *Poetics*. Instead, he constructed a materialist aesthetics subject to citation and reproduction. He conceptualized theater in terms of cognition, rather than emotional intervention, laying the foundations for theatrical semiology (per Barthes, "his theater is neither pathetic nor cerebral: it is justified theater"[39]). His technique is oriented on dialectical *interruption* of (the illusion of) art as (a mirror of) false consciousness. Louis Althusser understood this dialectic more profoundly than most. In his essay "The 'Piccolo Teatro': Bertolazzi and Brecht" he traced how the A-effect (*distanciation*, in French) is produced and represented in Brecht's *Mother Courage*, in the dynamics of its internal structure, including its temporal structure, offering as well a critique of the illusions of consciousness and a revelation of its real conditions.[40] And just as the play includes no "Last Judgement" of its own "story" (a "story" that is never concluded), the spectator, too:

...sees and lives the play in the mode of a questioned false consciousness. For what else is he if not the brother of the characters, caught in the spontaneous myths of ideology, in its illusions and privileged forms, as much as they are? If he is kept at a distance from the play by the play itself, it is not to spare him or to set him up as a Judge—on the contrary, it is to take him and enlist him in this apparent distance, in this 'estrangement'—to make him into this distance itself, the distance which is simply an active and living critique.[41]

In paradoxical fashion, Althusser's reading brings him to a mimetic, cathartic *gestus* that repeats Brecht's (and prefigures Prigov's):

Yes, like Mother Courage, we have the same war at our gates, and a handsbreadth from us, if not in us, the same horrible blindness, the same dust in our eyes, the same earth in our mouths. We have the same dawn and night, we skirt the same abysses: our unconsciousness. We even share the same history—and that is how it all started. That is why we were already ourselves in the play itself, from the beginning—and then what does it matter whether we know the result, since it will never happen to anyone but ourselves, that is, still in our world.[42]

Golem Soveticus

> According to the script I was the Golem Soveticus—a metaphor
> and metonymy of the structurally complex phenomenon of the
> Soviet state and the Soviet existence as stewards and heirs of
> the Russian religious-apocalyptic consciousness, of traditions
> of the European Enlightenment, and of the massoid-urban
> reconfiguration of European society in the twentieth century.
> [...] Yes, people are prone to give birth to monsters that then
> turn around and take possession of them. To be precise, they
> extract and intensify parts of themselves, imposing these
> creations on themselves as their own true purpose and being.
> —Dmitri Alexandrovich Prigov, *Golem*[43]

Prigov's priceless contribution to "sovietology" consists in
his comprehension of "Soviet existence" not as a radical,
irreversible revolution or rupture, but as the "steward-
ship" and "inheritance" of three traditions, or of three
paradigms: the Russian religious consciousness, rushing
towards the end of the world; European Enlightenment;
and the "reconfiguration" of European society in the twen-
tieth century (encompassing the revolt of the masses, total
mobilization, permanent scientific-technical revolution,
etc.). This symbiosis is indeed monstrous, but nevertheless
"the Soviet sociocultural project was not the efflorescence
on earth of some form of alien consciousness and alien
state of being; rather, it was embedded in the very nature
of humanity."[44]

For this reason, with regard to Prigov, one may declare
precisely the same thing that Gogol asserted with regards
to Pushkin as Russian national poet, replacing the word

"Russian" with "Soviet" (in this novel, Prigovian, meaning). As Gogol claimed for Pushkin in relation to Russian culture, we may conclude that in truth, Prigov is an extraordinary manifestation, perhaps even the sole manifestation, of the Soviet spirit: here is Soviet man at the stage of development he will perhaps reach two hundred years hence.* Soviet nature, the Soviet soul, the Soviet language, the Soviet character are reflected in him with the same purity, the same purified beauty, with which a landscape is reflected by the convex surface of an optical lens. And so on and so forth, as in the original text.[45]

* In every joke there is an element of joke. Didn't DAP realize, on his own sublime level, the communist utopia as it is described in *The German Ideology*, in which the elimination of the division of labor makes it possible, in Marx's famous formulation, "to hunt in the morning, catch fish after noon, turn to animal husbandry in the evening, and devote oneself to criticism in the evening," as well as to poetry, prose, installation and video art, and other forms of self-improvement?

References

Bibliographic references to publications in Russian utilize the accepted Library of Congress Transliteration system, which results in slightly different forms than those used in the main text ("Dmitrii" rather then "Dmitry" or "Dmitri").

1 Boris Paramonov, "Poslednii velikii poet sovetskoi epokhi" ["The last great poet of the Soviet era"], *NG-EX LIBRIS*, 19 July 2007.

2 Prigov's passion for numerology, for the determination of all sorts of numbers ("the general German number" "the Blok number") is well known. Prigov's "murderous consistency of formal cognition," his comprehension of the poetic word as "an element of a certain logical construction," is a central concern in the correspondence between Igor Smirnov and Boris Groys: "Subject: Prigov (perepisyvaius' s Borisom Groisom)," *Filosofiia na kazhdyi den'* (Moscow: Pragmatika kul'tury, 2003).

3 Mikhail Bakhtin's work on Rabelais and the Medieval culture of laughter was published in 1965. Given its enormous resonance in the Soviet cultural milieu, it's unlikely that it escaped Prigov's attention. In any case, the atmosphere of ambivalence, travesty, carnival crowning and dethroning, and (Medieval) eschatology with its "cosmic fear" is a pervasive presence in Prigov.

4 Igor Smirnov, "Byt i bytie v stikhakh D. A. Prigova" ["Everyday life and existence in the poetry of D. A. Prigov"], *Nekanonicheskii klassik: Dmitrii Aleksandrovich Prigov (1940–2007): sbornik statei i materialov*, ed. E. Dobrenko, M. Lipovetskii, I. Kukulin, and M. Maiofis (Moscow: NLO, 2010), 96-105.

5 See: Dmitrii Golynko-Vol'fson, "Chitaia Prigova: neodno-znachnaia i neochevidnaia" ["Reading Prigov: the equivocal and the unobvious"], *Novoe literaturnoe obozrenie*, 2007, No. 87, 289. Georg Witte and Sabine Hänsgen view Prigov's serial method

from another, existential-metaphysical angle, writing in the same set of memorial publications in the *New Literary Observer*: "This serial creation of texts, something like an assembly line, is just a parodic imitation of the mechanisms of automated production. It's an existential act, a survival strategy, filling in the enormous, threatening sink-hole of metaphysical vacuum with masses and ever more masses of texts." See their "O nemetskoi poeticheskoi knige Dmitriia Aleksandrovicha Prigova 'Der Milizionär und die Anderen'" ["About Dmitri Alexandrovich Prigov's German Book 'Der Milizionär und die Anderen'"], *Novoe literaturnoe obozrenie*, 2007, No. 87, 295.

6   Andy Warhol, "What Is Pop Art? Interview by G. R. Swenson," *Art News*, Volume 62, Number 7, 1963, 26.

7   Bertolt Brecht, *Threepenny Novel*, trans. by Desmond I. Vesey and Christopher Isherwood (New York: Grove Press, 1956), 172. In the original "blunt thought" is "plumpes Danken."

8   D. A. Prigov, "Iskusstvo segodnia zanimaetsia ne soderzhaniem, a novymi tipami khudozhestvennogo povedeniia" ["Art today is oriented not on content, but on new types of artistic behavior"], *Russkii zhurnal*, April 16, 2007, www.russ.ru/Mirovaya-povestka/Iskusstvo-segodnya-zanimaetsya-ne-soderzhaniem-a-novymi-tipami-hudozhestvennogo-povedeniya (accessed September 14, 2019).

9   D. A. Prigov, "I pozhrala... no ne do kontsa! Ne do kontsa?" ["And she ate it... but not entirely! Not entirely?"], *Novoe literaturnoe obozrenie*, 2007, No. 87, 322.

10   D. A. Prigov and S. I. Shapoval, *Portretnaia galereia D.A.P.* [*D.A.P.'s Portrait Gallery*] (Moscow: NLO, 2003), 118.

11   Ibid, p. 20.

12   Harold Rosenberg, *Art On the Edge: Creators and Situations* (Chicago: University of Chicago Press, 1983), 98.

13   Prigov and Shapoval, *Portretnaia galereia*, 21.

14   Klaus Honnef, *Andy Warhol, 1928-1987: Commerce Into Art* (Cologne: Taschen, 1993), 38. Honnef is the author of a book on Pop Art in the same series.

15   Ibid, 54.

16   Charles Baudelaire, "Fusées," *Oeuvres complètes*, Paris: Pléiade, Gallimard, 1975), I: 662.

17   Walter Benjamin, from the essay "Central Park," translated by Edmund Jephcott and Howard Eiland, in *The Writer of Modern Life: Essays on Charles Baudelaire*, ed. by Michael W. Jennings (Cambridge, Mass.: Harvard University Press, 2006), 142.

18   Prigov's early poetry can be found at: "Russkaia poeziia 1960-kh" ["Russian poetry of the 1960s"], http://www.ruthenia.ru/60s/prigov/index.htm (accessed September 14, 2019).

19   The two poems are "Moi druz'ia s obidoiu i zharom…," from the *4-i rukopisnyi sbornik "Stikhotvorenii,"* and "I etot mne protiven…" from the book *Russkoe*. Cited in A. Zholkovskii, *Bluzhdaiushchie sny i drugie raboty* [*Wandering Dreams and Other Works*] (Moscow: Nauka–Vostochnaia literatura, 1994), 54-70.

20   Cited in Kristen Ross, *The Emergence of Social Space: Rimbaud and the Paris Commune* (Minneapolis: University of Minnesota Press, 1988), 26. In the introduction to the Russian edition of Lautréamont's works, Georgii Kosikov writes, that "In both thematic and stylistic terms, the *Songs of Maldoror* is artic-ulated as a collection of 'common places' of European literature,

artfully recombined by the narrator, who furthermore continuously shies away from uttering his own 'word about the world.' If Mikhail Bakhtin were in need of an adequate example of a work in which not only is there no 'unified language and style,' but in which even the author 'emerges without direct speech of his own" and simply occupies 'the organizational center for the intersection of planes,' the *Songs of Maldoror* could serve as a truly excellent illustration." In: Lotreamon, *Pesni Mal'dorora. Stikhotvoreniia. Lotreamon posle Lotreamona* (Moscow: Ad Marginem, 1998), 46.

21   Prigov and Shapoval, *Portretnaia galereia*, 30.

22   Roland Barthes, "Literature and Signification," in his *Critical Essays*, trans. by Richard Howard (Evanston, Ill.: Northwestern University Press, 1972), 263-64.

23   Bertolt Brecht, *Bertolt Brecht's Me-Ti: Book of Interventions In the Flow of Things*, ed. and trans. by Antony Tatlow (London: Bloomsbury, 2016), 75.

24   Bertolt Brecht, *Brecht on Art and Politics*, ed. by Tom Kuhn and Steve Giles, trans. by Laura Bradley, Steve Giles and Tom Kuhn (London: Methuen, 2003), 45.

25   I. Fradkin, "Tvorcheskii put' Brekhta—dramaruga" ["Brecht's Creative Path as a Playwright"] in: Bertol't Brekht, *Teatr. P'esy. Stat'i. Vyskazyvaniia. V Piati tomakh*, vol. I (Moscow Iskusstvo, 1963), cited via the electronic edition at https://www.rulit.me/books/stihotvoreniya-rasskazy-pesy-read-398876-3.html (accessed September 21, 2019).

26   From the *Lyceum*, fragment 108. Friedrich Schlegel, *Dialogue on Poetry and Literary Aphorisms*, translated and edited by Ernst Behler and Roman Strug (University Park: Penn State University Press, 1968), 131.

27   D. A. Prigov, *Sovetskie teksty* [*Soviet Texts*] (Saint-Petersburg: Izdatel'stvo Ivana Limbakha, 1997), 215.

28   Ian Satunovskii, *Sredi bela dnia* [*In Broad Daylight*], (Moscow: OGI, 2001), 55.

29   Patrice Pavis, *Dictionary of the Theatre: Terms, Concepts, and Analysis*, trans. by Christine Shantz (Toronto, Canada: University of Toronto Press, 1998), 19.

30   On the genesis of the A-effect, see the chapter "Verfremdung: *Brecht's Estrangement Theory*" in Douglas Robinson, *Estrangement and the Somatics of Literature: Tolstoy, Shklovsky, Brecht* (The Johns Hopkins University Press, 2008), 176-257.

31   Barthes, "Literature and Signification," 263.

32   Dmitrii Prigov, "Ogranichennost' inovatsii" ["The Limited Nature of Innovation"], *Soobshcheniia*, 2004, No. 1, http://soob.ru/n/2004/1/concept/4 (accessed September 21, 2019).

33   Bertolt Brecht, *Brecht on Theater: The Development of an Aesthetic*, ed. and trans. by John Willett (New York: Hill and Wang, 1964), 136-139. For consistency, I have adjusted Willett's use of "gest" in translating "gestus" back to Brecht's original term. [KP]

34   From the "Appendices to the Messingkauf Theory," in: Bertolt Brecht, *The Messingkauf Dialogues*, trans. by John Willett (London: Methuen, 1965), 104.

35   The first poem is reproduced from the Prigov subpage on the site "Russkaia poeziia 1960–kh," http://www.ruthenia.ru/60s/prigov/index.htm (accessed September 21, 2019). The second is from Prigov, *Sovetskie teksty*, 39.

36   Prigov and Shapoval, *Portretnaia galereia*, 104.

37   Ibid, 94.

38   Ibid, 96.

39   Barthes, "Literature and Signification," 262.

40   Louis Althusser, *For Marx*, trans. by Ben Brewster (London: Verso, 2005), 146-47.

41   Ibid, 148.

42   Ibid, 150.

43   From the script for "Good-bye, USSR," that was performed at the Frankfurt Book Fair in 2003, published in *Novoe literaturnoe obozrenie*, 2007, No. 87. 316-318. Besides Prigov, the participants of the performance included Grisha Bruskin (in the role of author-producer), Lev Rubinshtein, Vladimir Tarasov and Irina Prokhorova.

44   Ibid, 318.

45   See N. V. Gogol, "A Few Words About Pushkin," trans. Lauren G. Leighton, *Canadian-American Slavic Studies* 29, Nos. 3-4 (1995), 395.

Note on the text

This translation is based on a text originally published as "Prigov kak Breht i Uorhol v odnom litse, ili Golem-soveticus," in an anthology of essays, *Nekanonicheskii klassik: Dmitrii Aleksandrovich Prigov (1940-2007) / Sbornik statei i materialov* (NLO, 2010), revised and reprinted in Aleksandr Skidan's essay collection, *Summa Poetiki* (NLO, 2016). A version is available on the "Chto Delat" website, chtodelat.org.

Golem Soveticus: Prigov as Brecht and Warhol in One Persona
© Aleksandr Skidan, 2020
Translation © Kevin M.F. Platt, 2020

2020 Pamphlet Series
ISBN 978-1-937027-89-6
First Edition, First Printing
Edition of 1,000

Ugly Duckling Presse
The Old American Can Factory
232 Third Street, #E-303
Brooklyn, NY 11215
uglyducklingpresse.org

Distributed in the USA by SPD/Small Press Distribution
Distributed in the UK by Inpress Books

Design by chuck kuan and Sarah Lawson
Typeset by Paige Parsons
Type is New Century Schoolbook
Cover paper and flyleaf from French Paper Co.
Printed offset and bound at McNaughton & Gunn
Flyleaf printed letterpress at Ugly Duckling Presse

This pamphlet is part of UDP's 2020 Pamphlet Series: twenty commissioned essays on poetics, translation, performance, collective work, pedagogy, and small press publishing. The authors are listed below; their pamphlets are available for individual purchase and as a subscription (uglyducklingpresse.org/subscribe). Each offers a different approach to the pamphlet as a form of working in the present, an engagement at once sustained and ephemeral.

Mirene Arsanios

Omar Berrada

Sergio Chejfec

Don Mee Choi

Kunci Study Forum & Collective

Iris Cushing

Simon Cutts

Nicole Cecilia Delgado

Adjua Gargi Nzinga Greaves

Dimitra Ioannou

Sibyl Kempson

Claudia La Rocco

Aditi Machado

Chantal Maillard

Tinashe Mushakavanhu

Sawako Nakayasu

Tammy Nguyen

Aleksandr Skidan

Steven Zultanski

Magdalena Zurawski

To win a subscription, write to office@uglyducklingpresse.org with your solution to the following puzzle: Using only 6 straight lines, divide the circle on the back cover so that each number is in its own section, without any overlap between numbers.